Your Name:

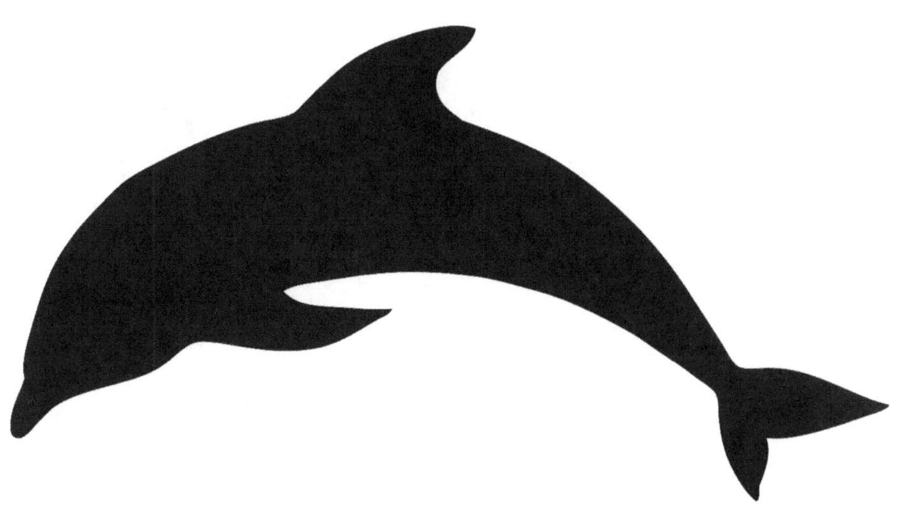

Daniel P. Santos

Dedication

This coloring book is dedicated to all the wonderful individuals who have purchased and enjoyed it. Your support and enthusiasm mean the world to me. May the pages of this book bring joy, creativity, and colorful adventures to your lives. Thank you for being a part of this journey.

With heartfelt appreciation,

Daniel P. Santos
2024

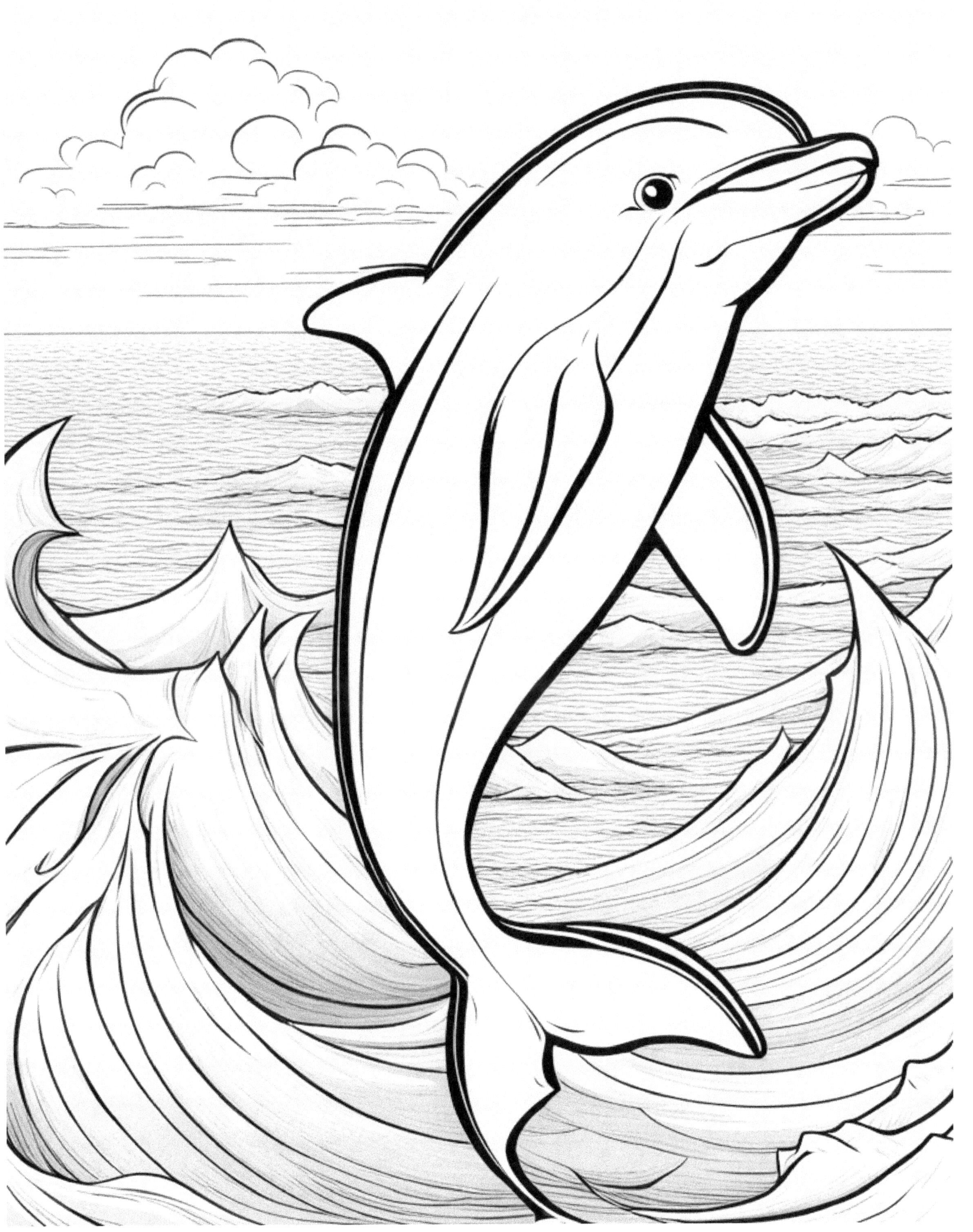

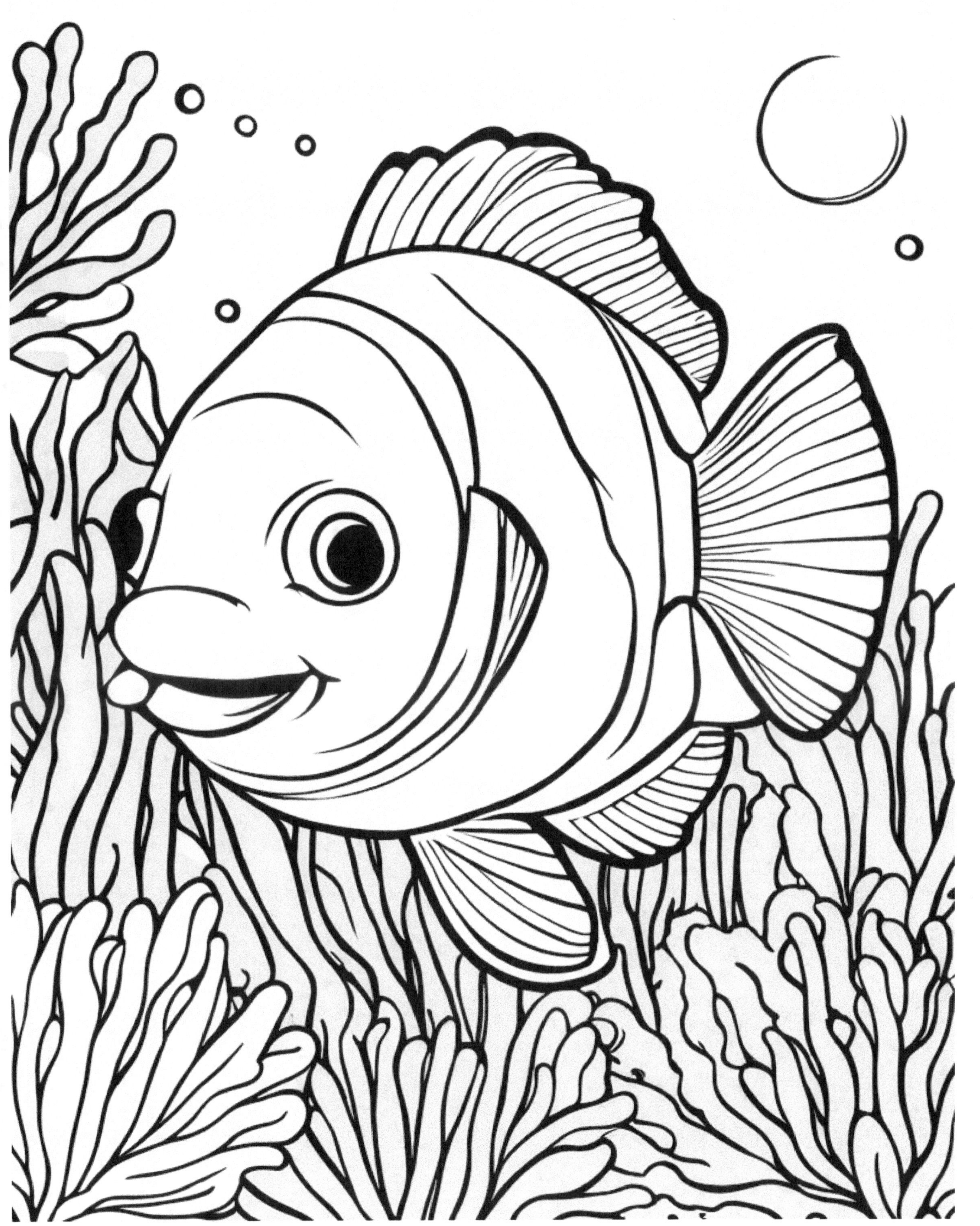

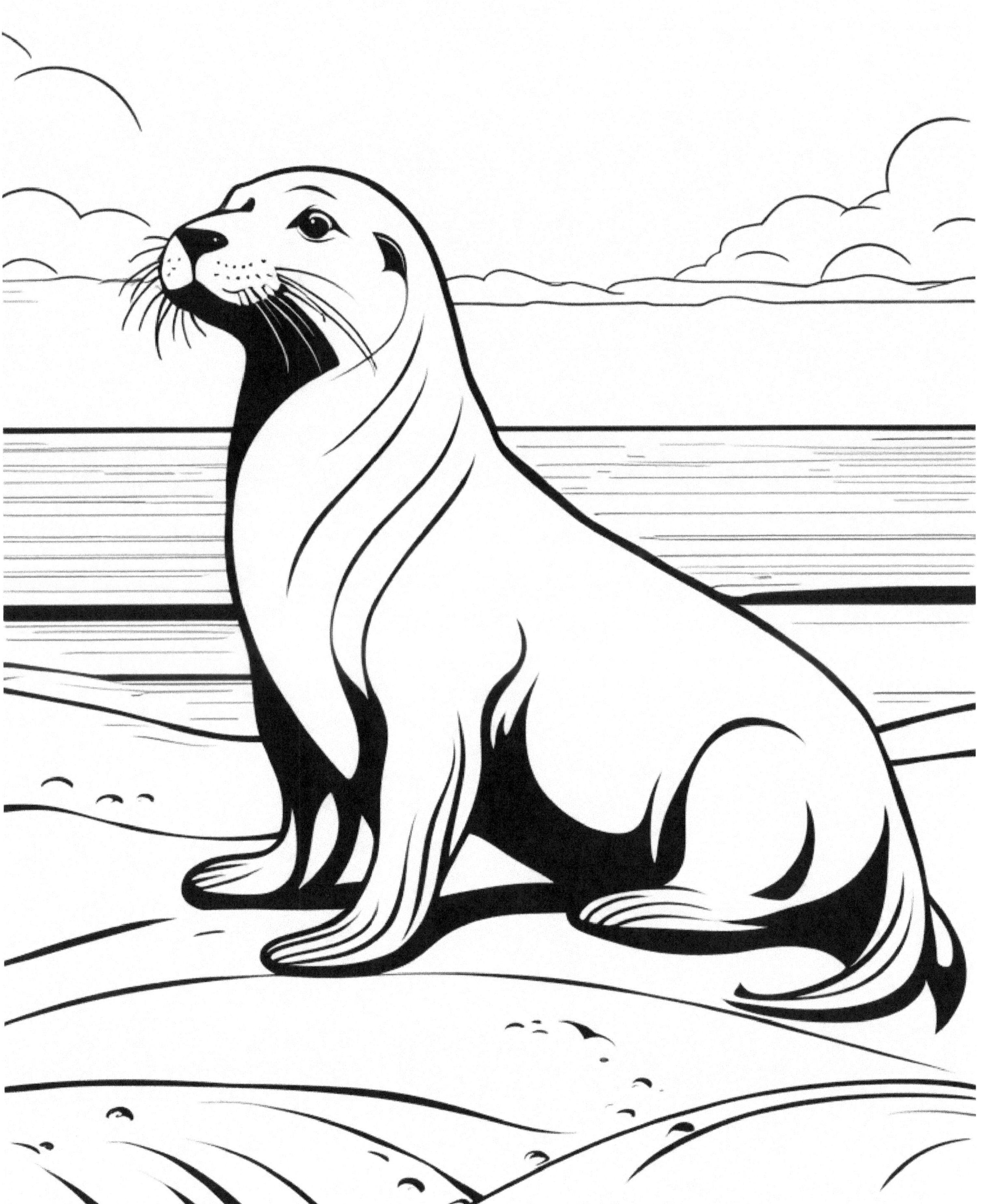

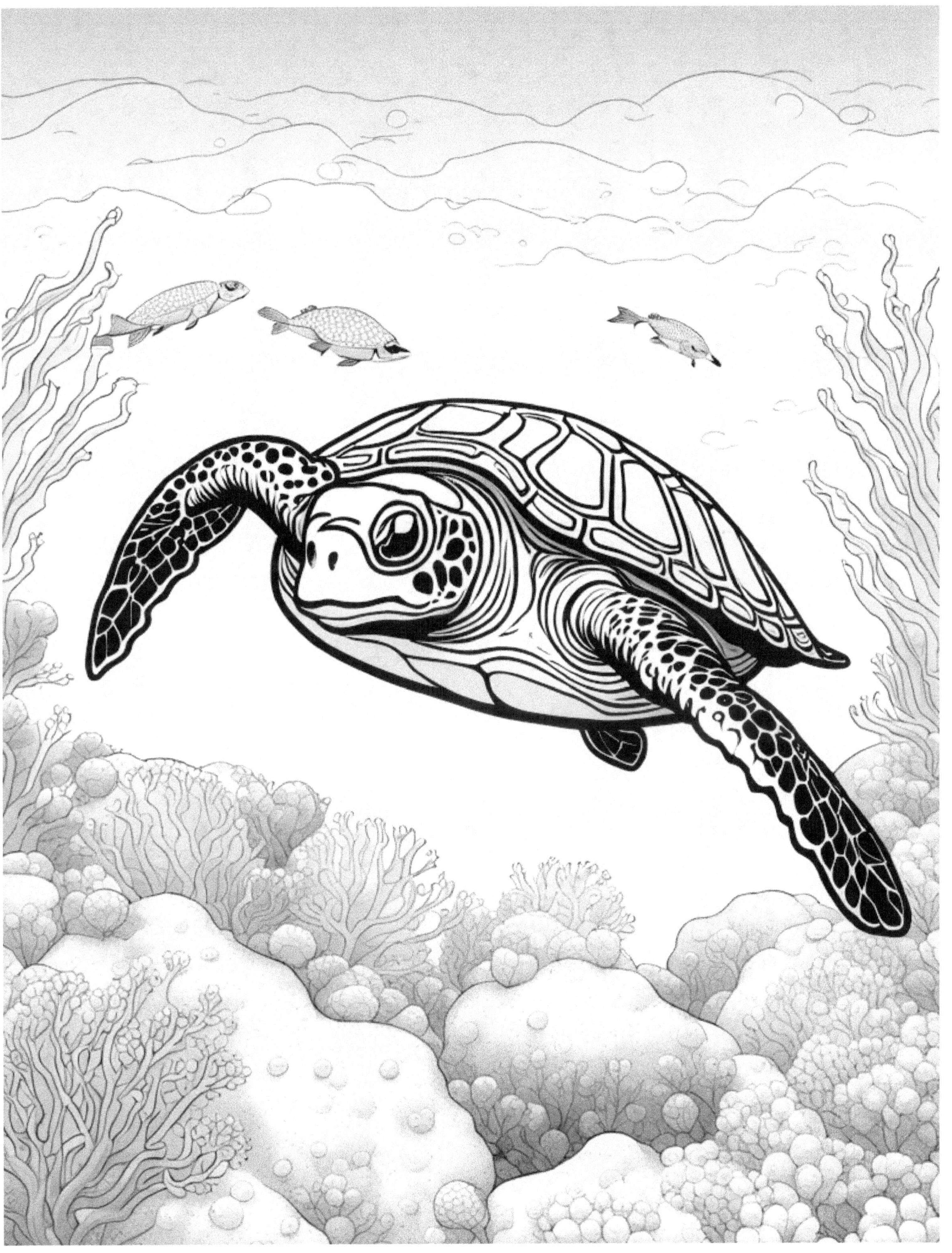

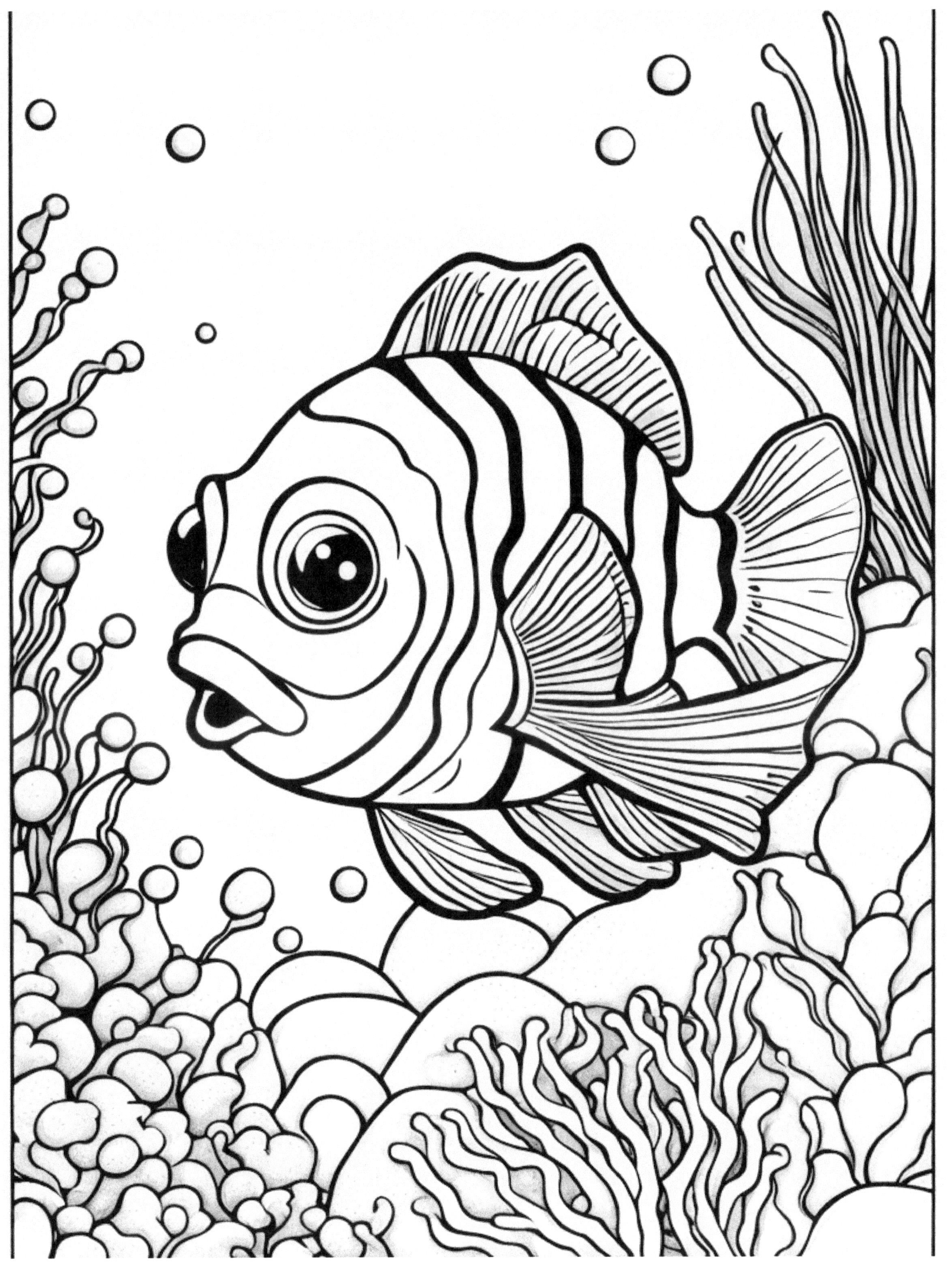

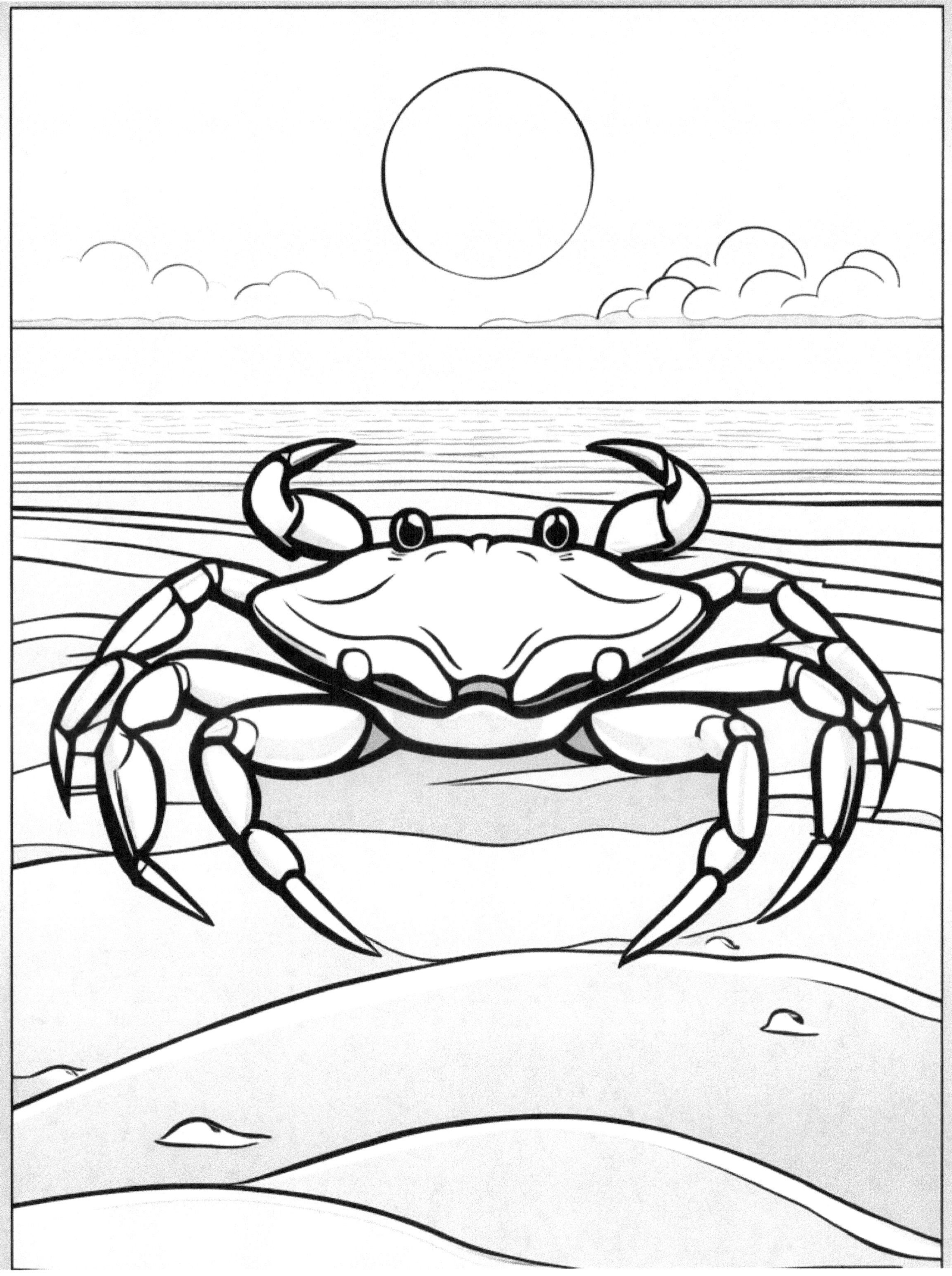

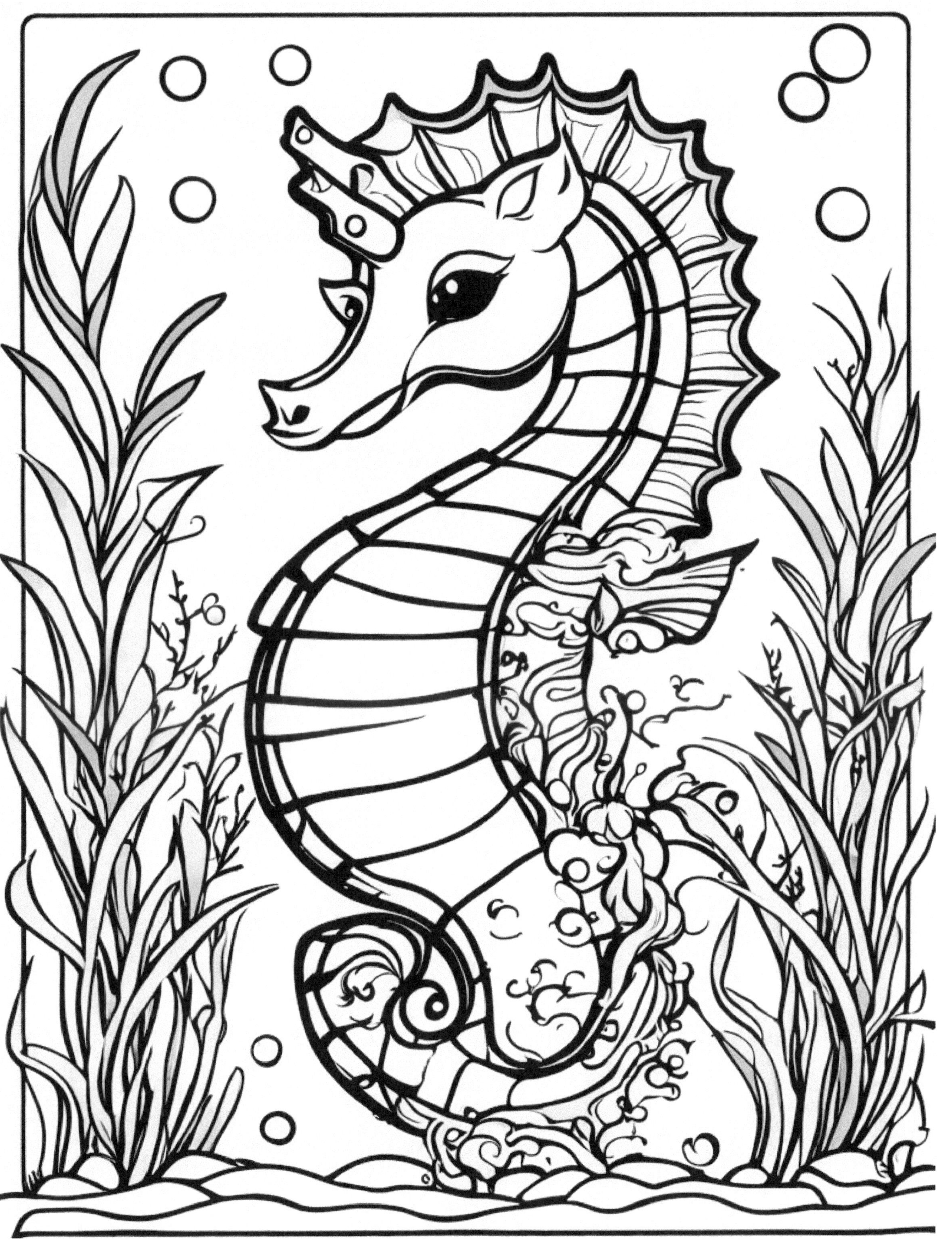

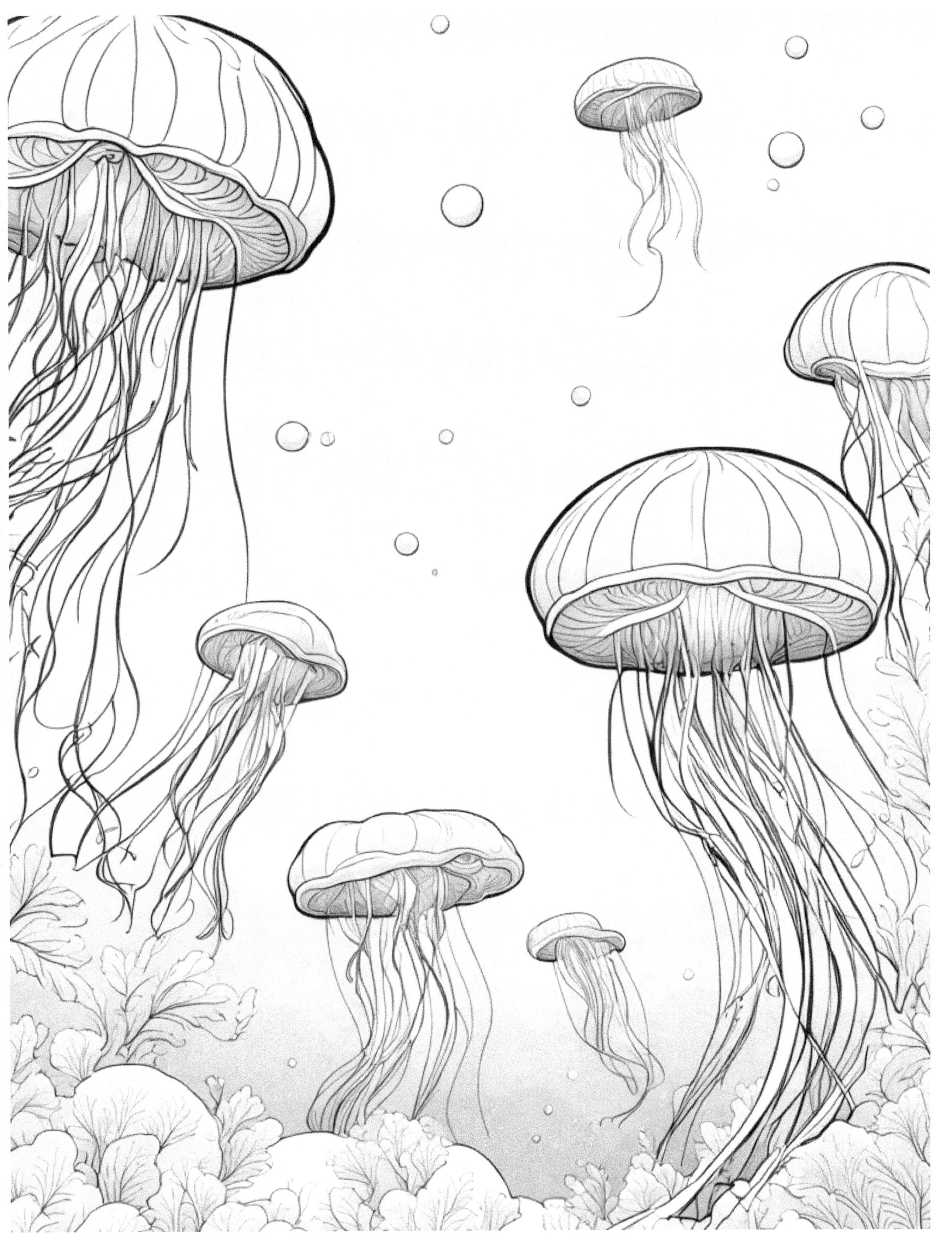

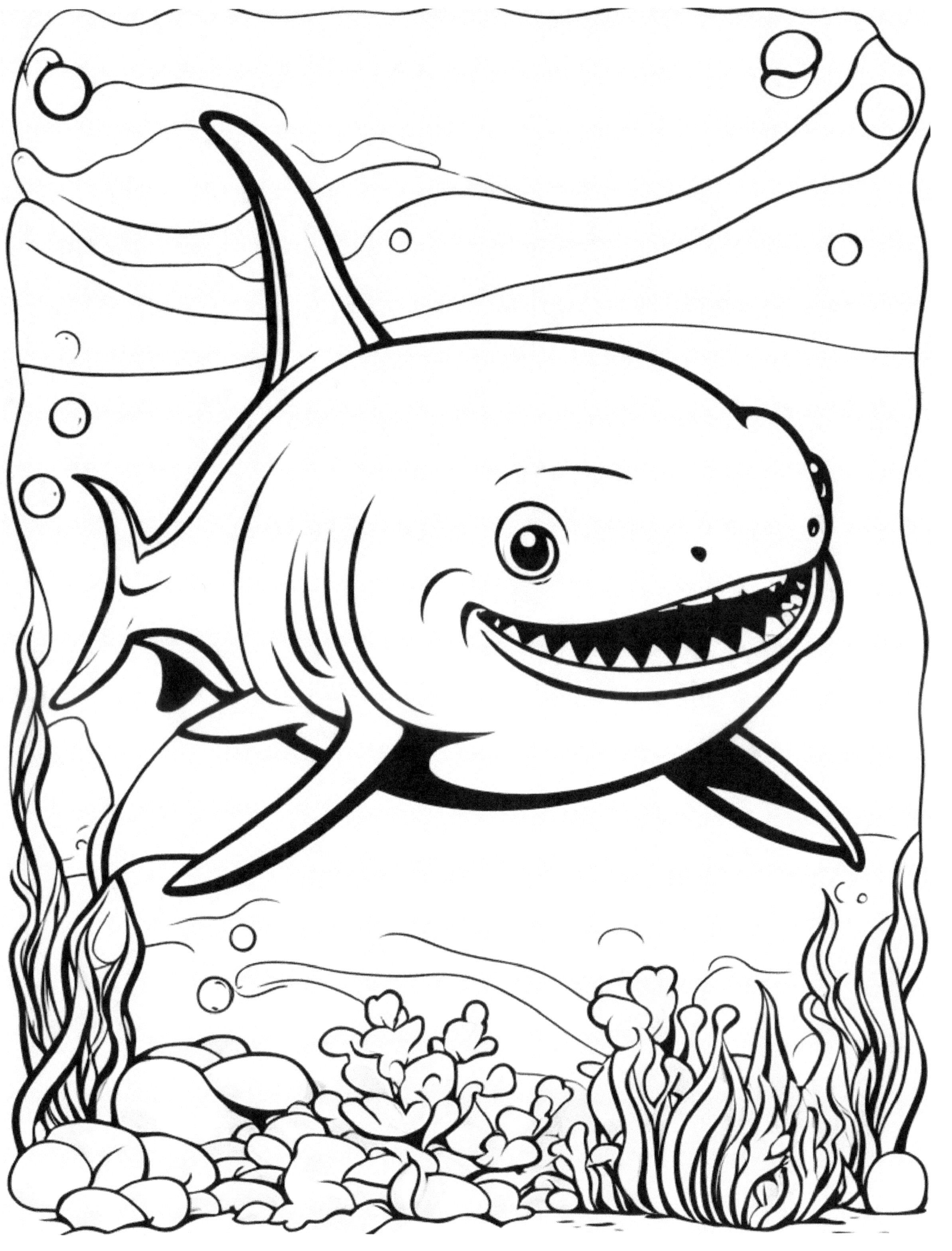

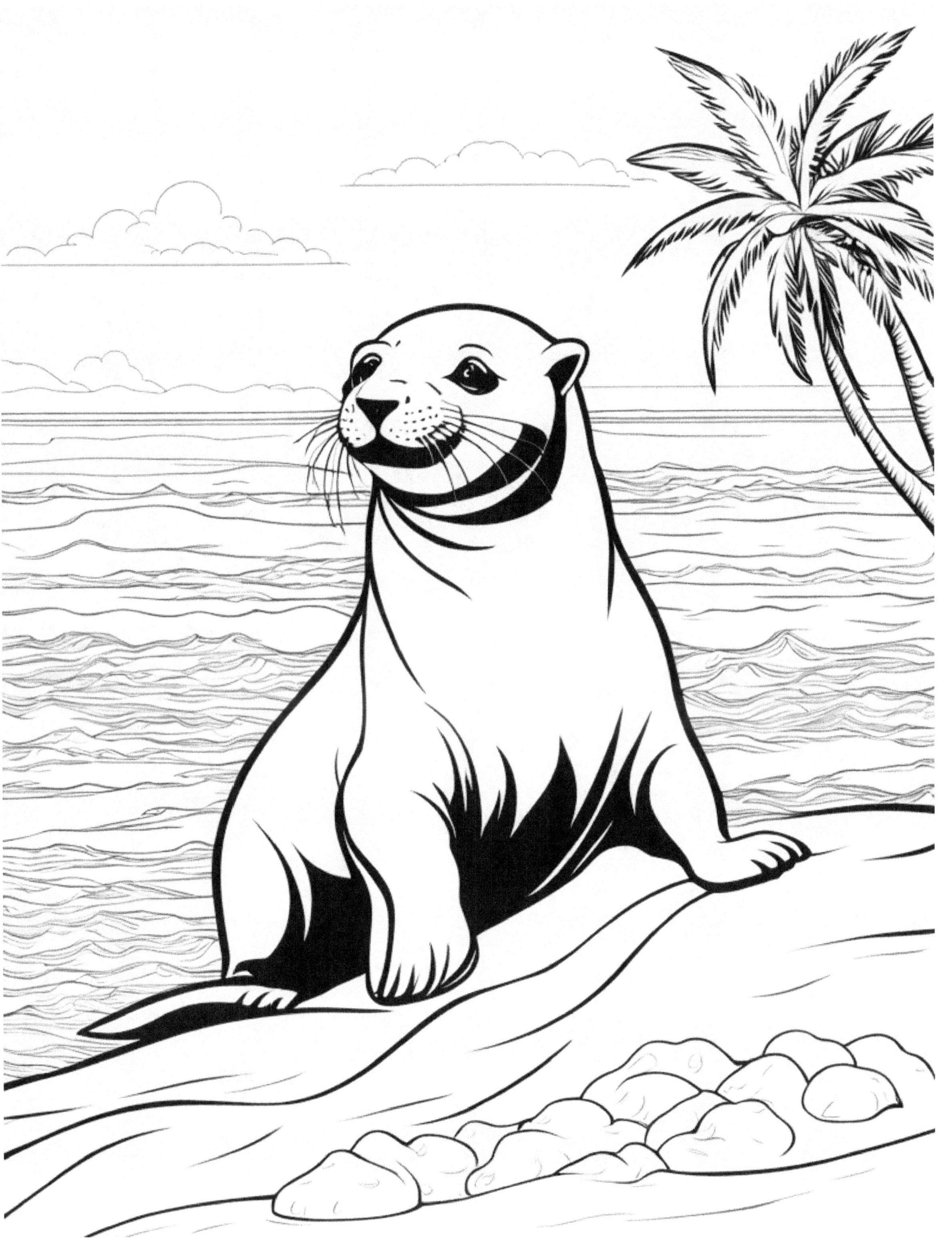

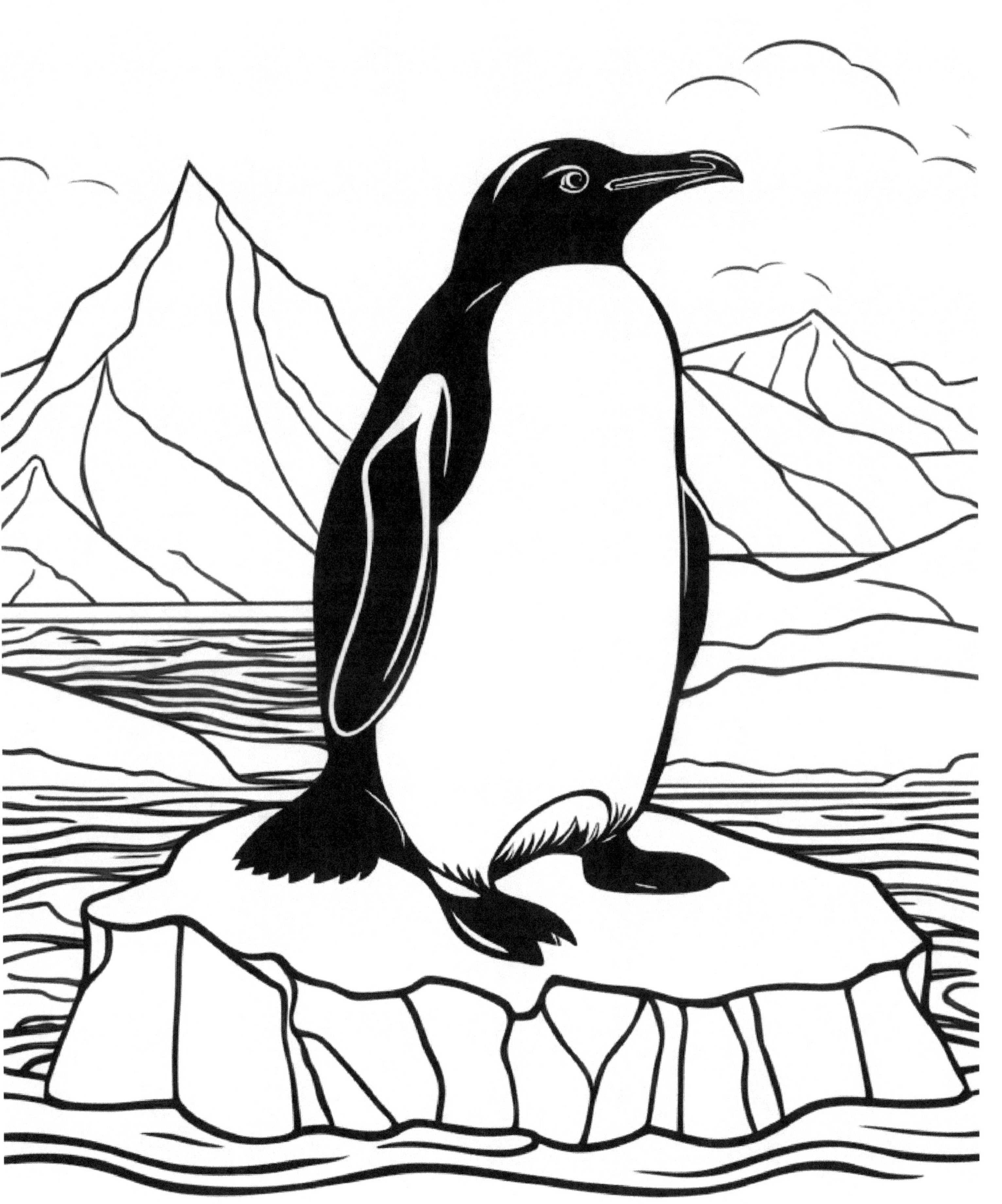

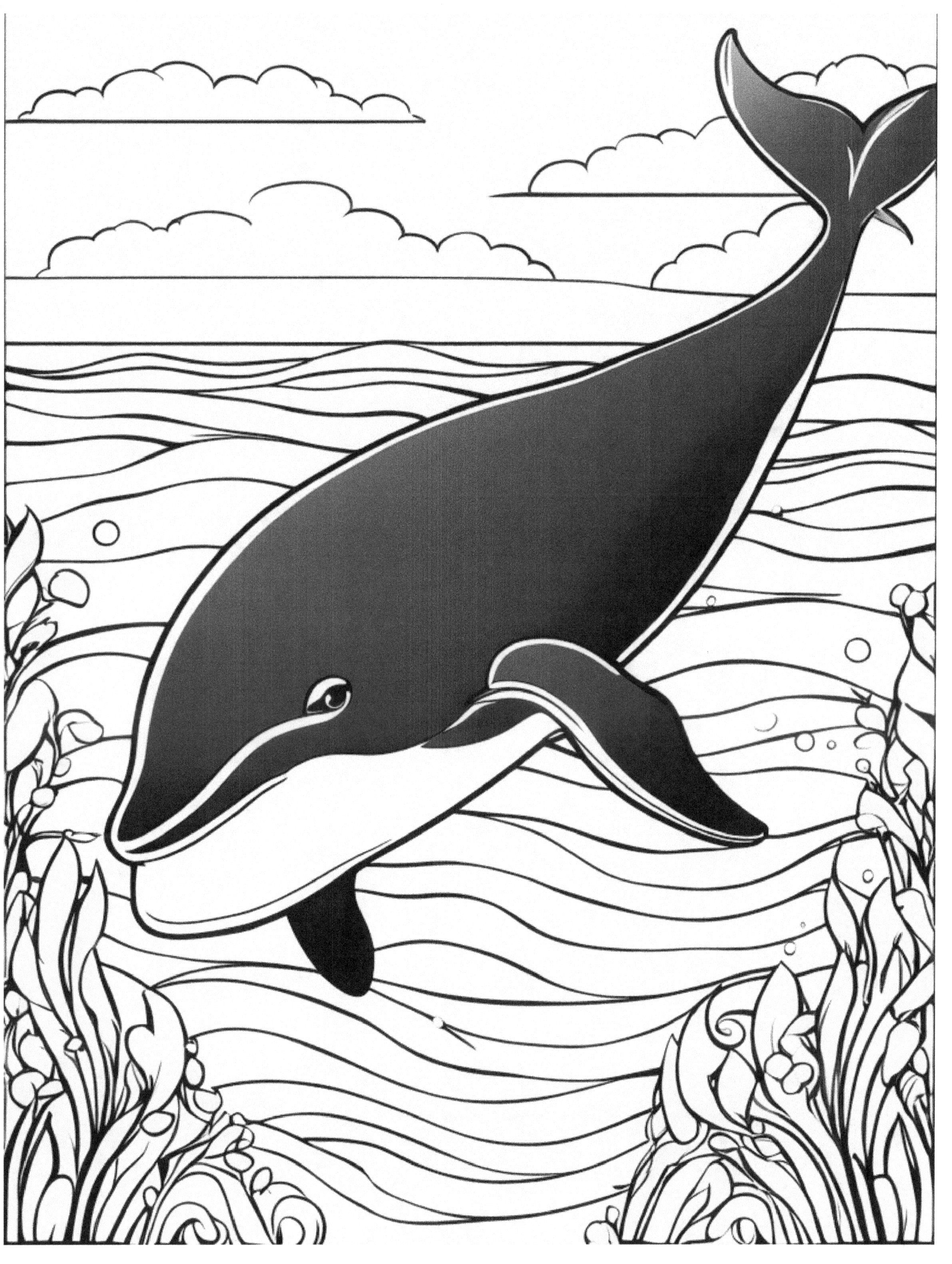

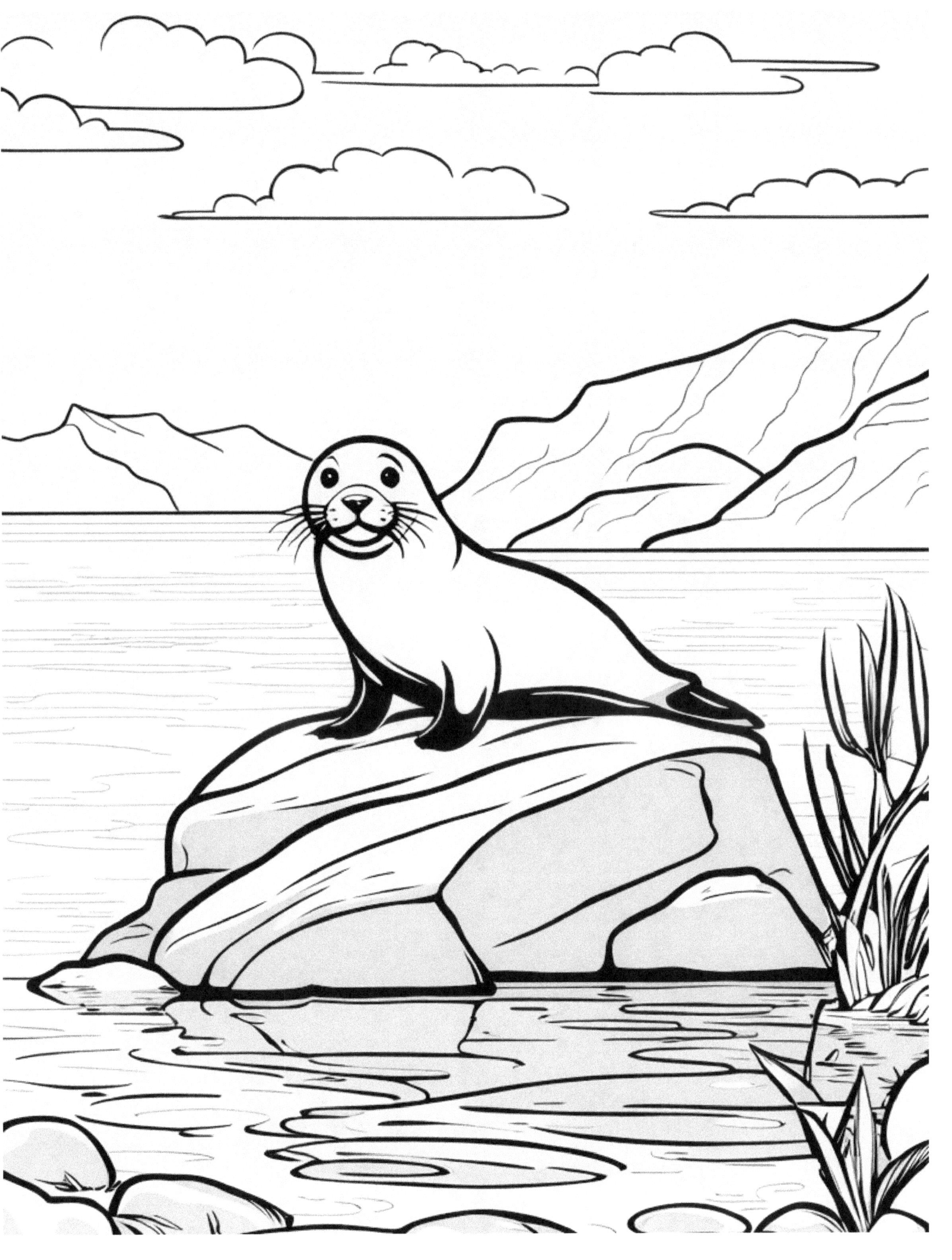

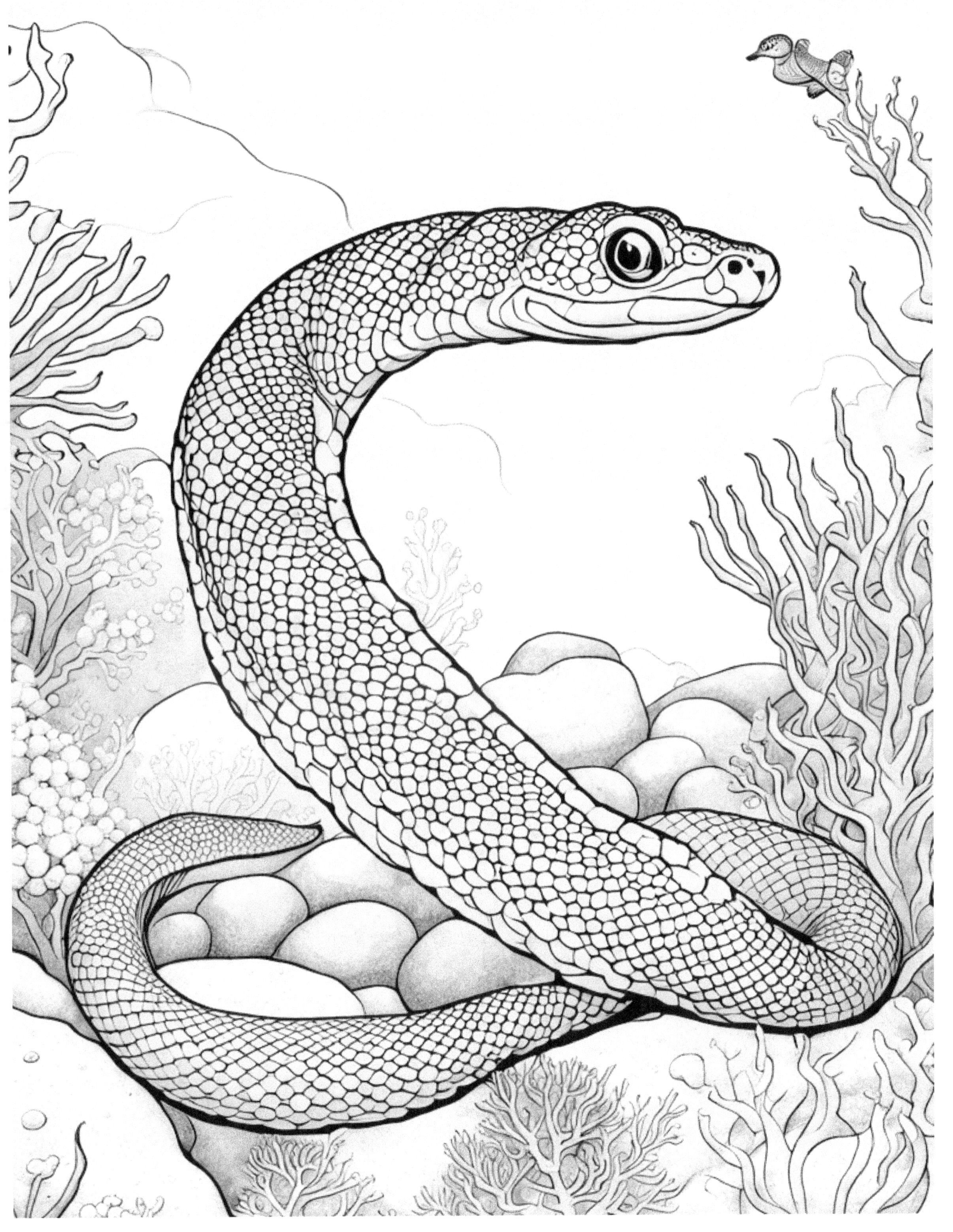

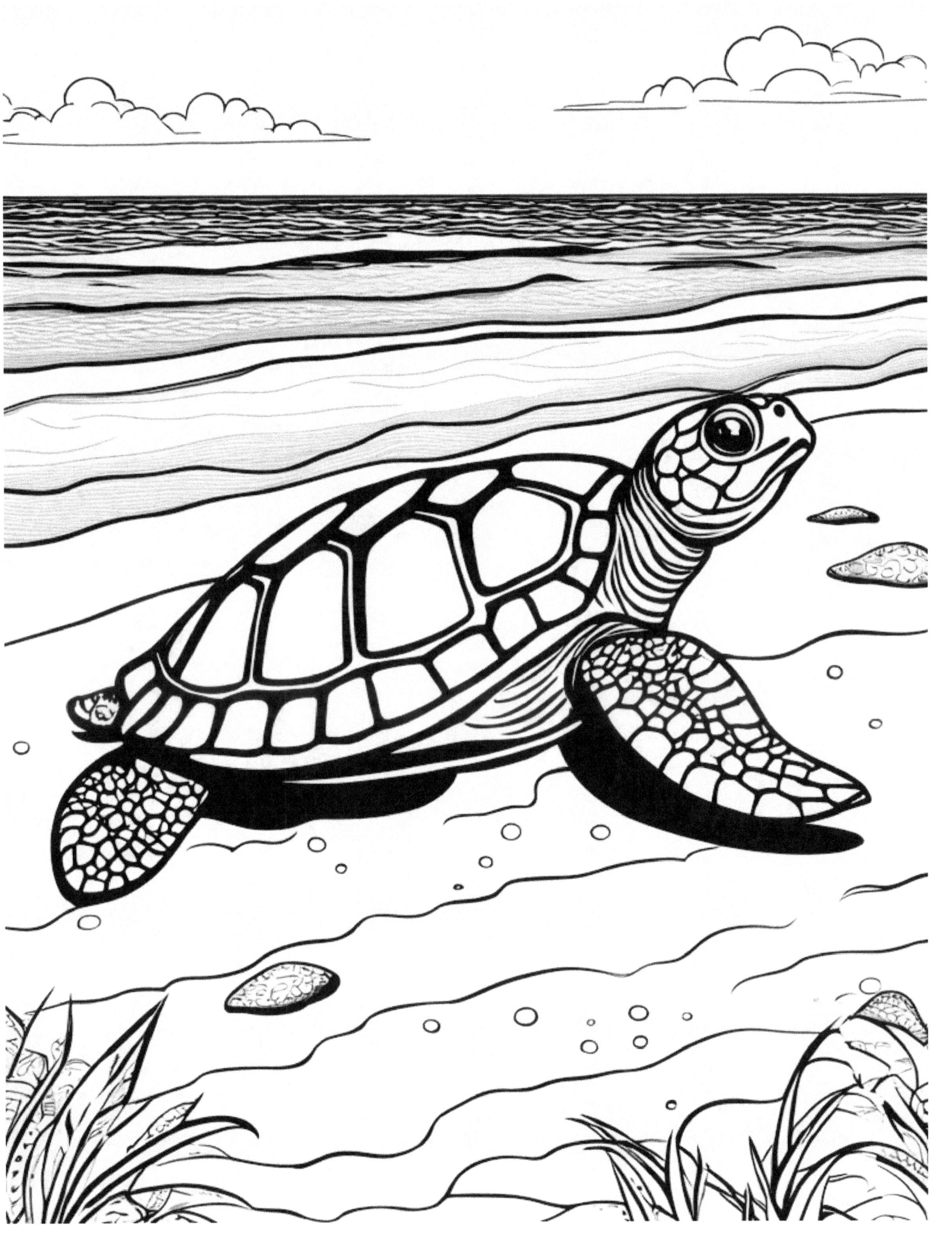

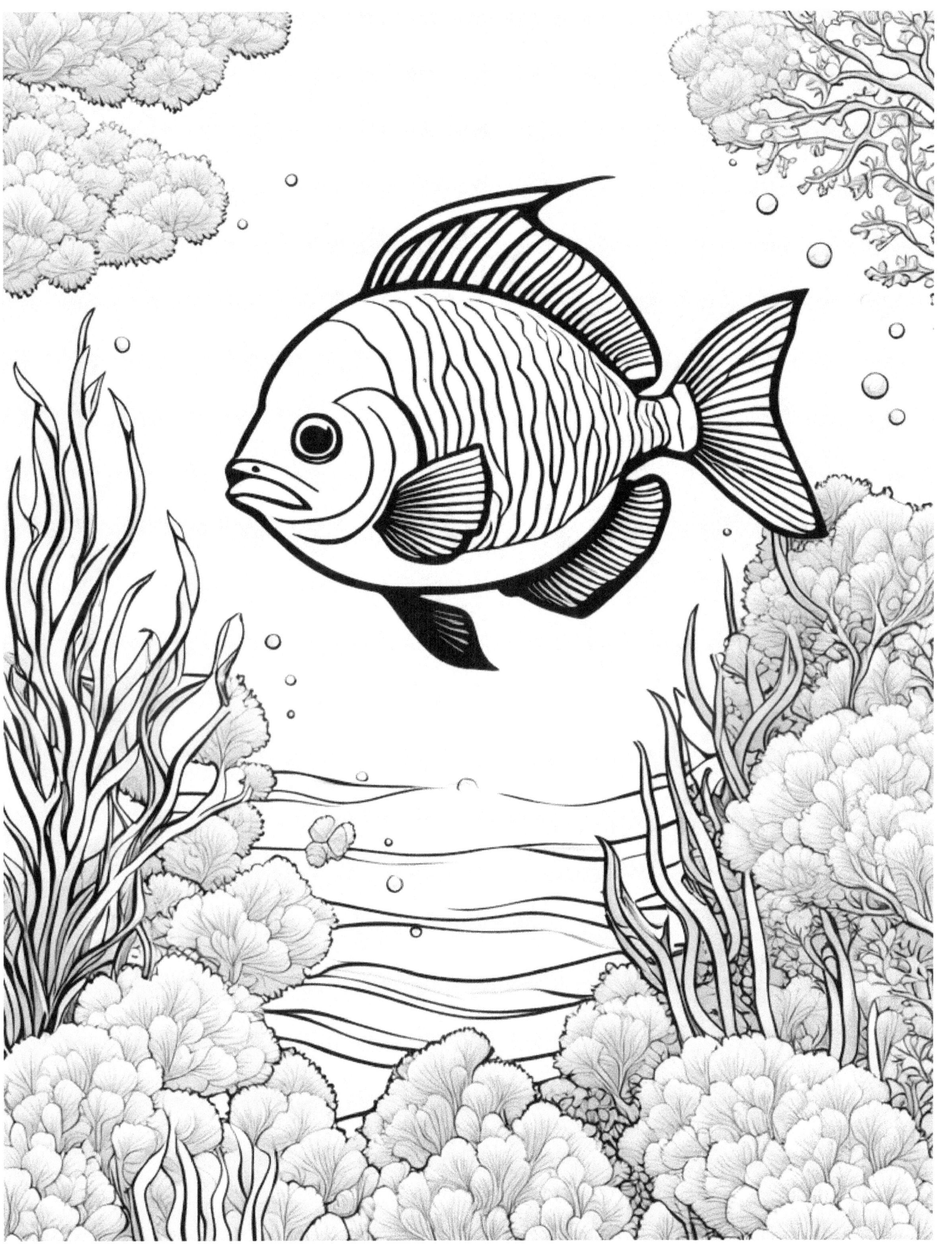

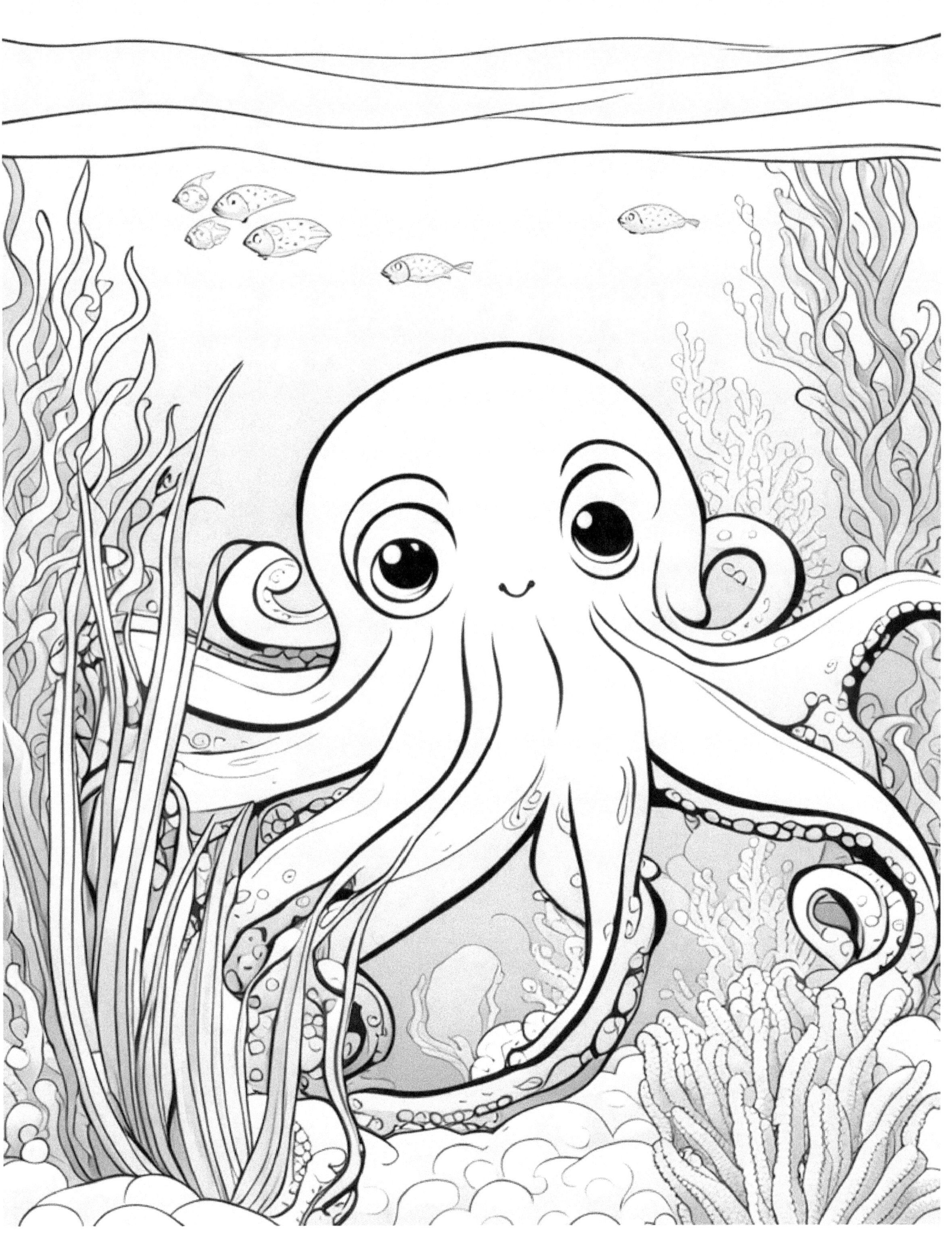

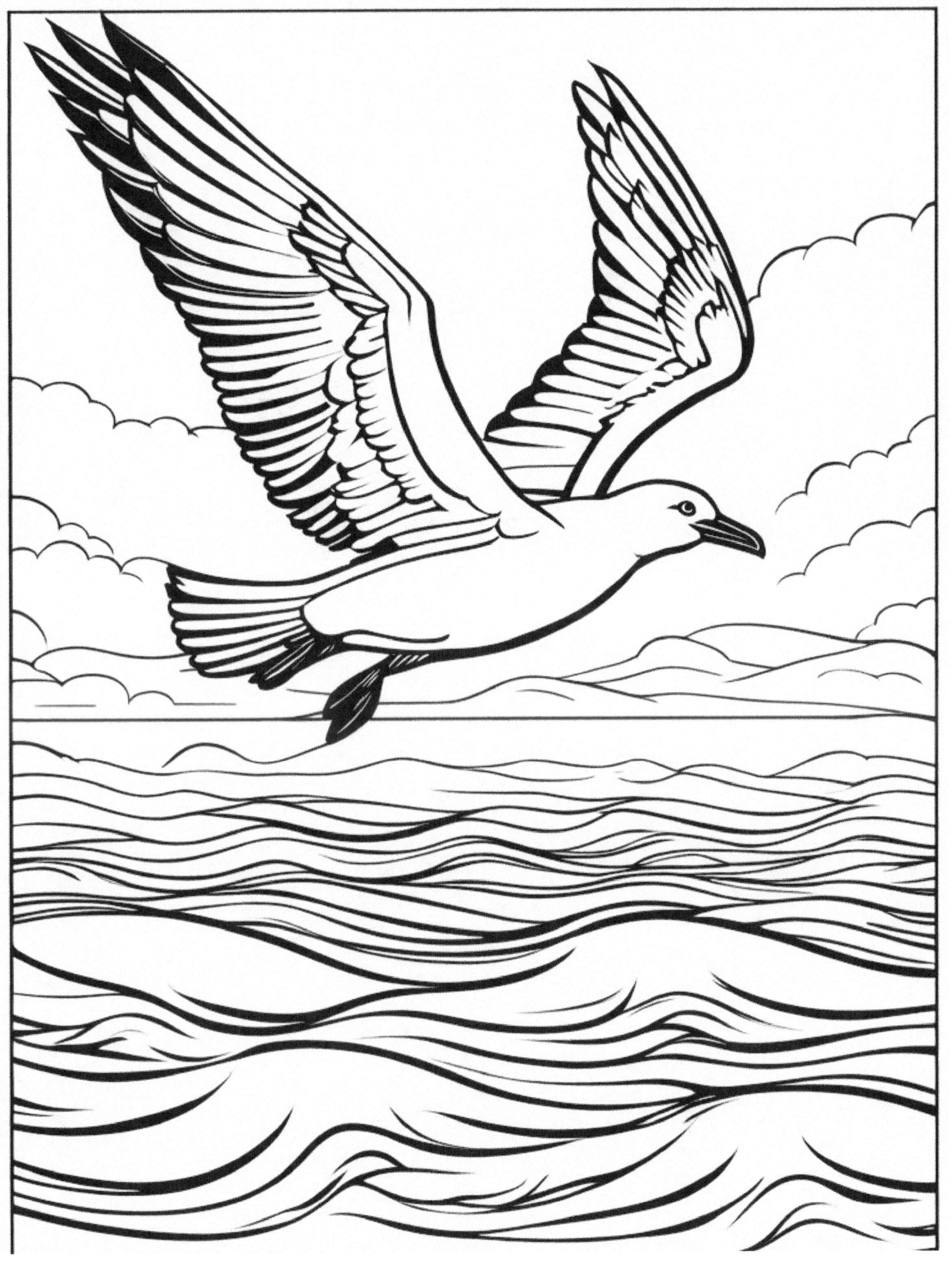

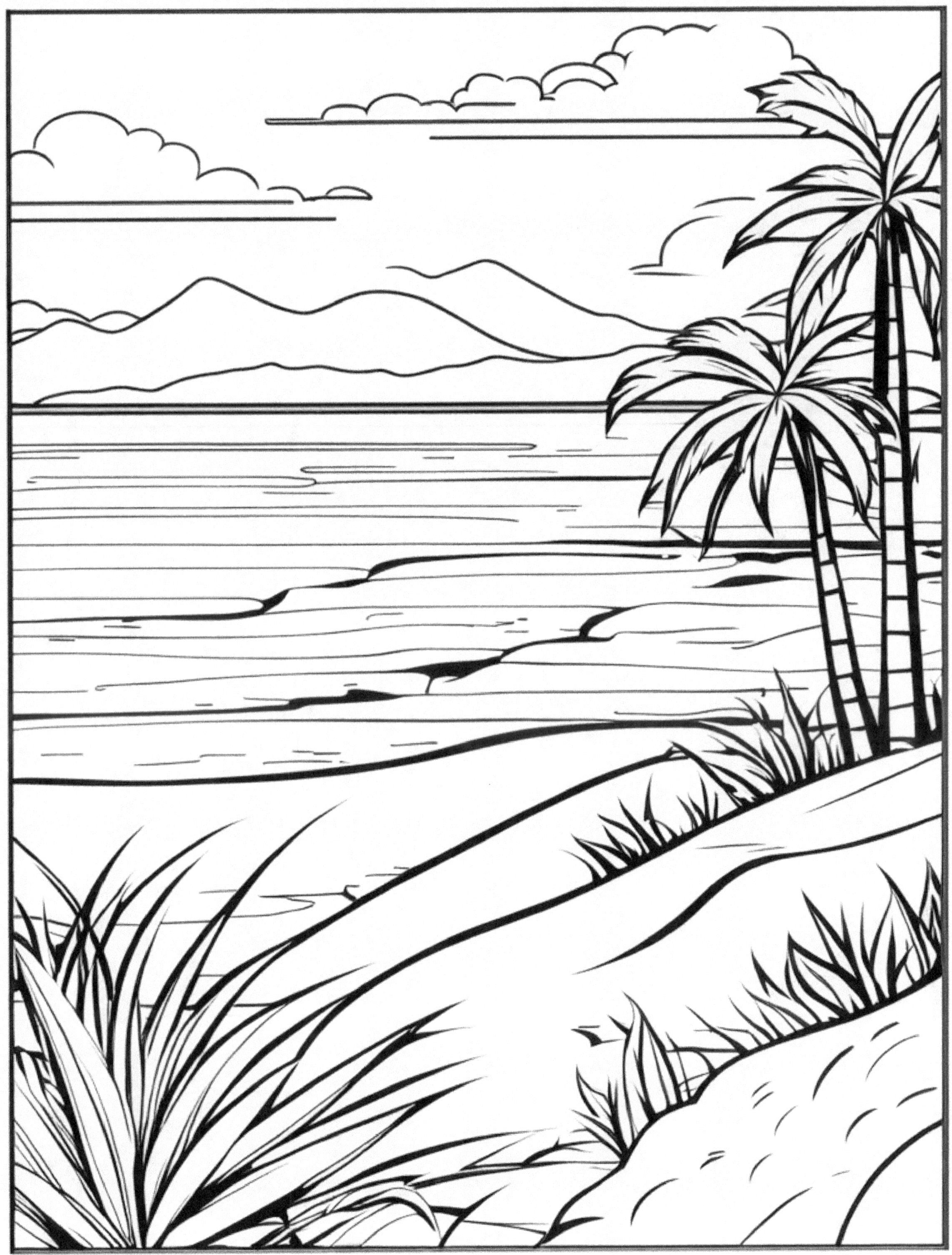

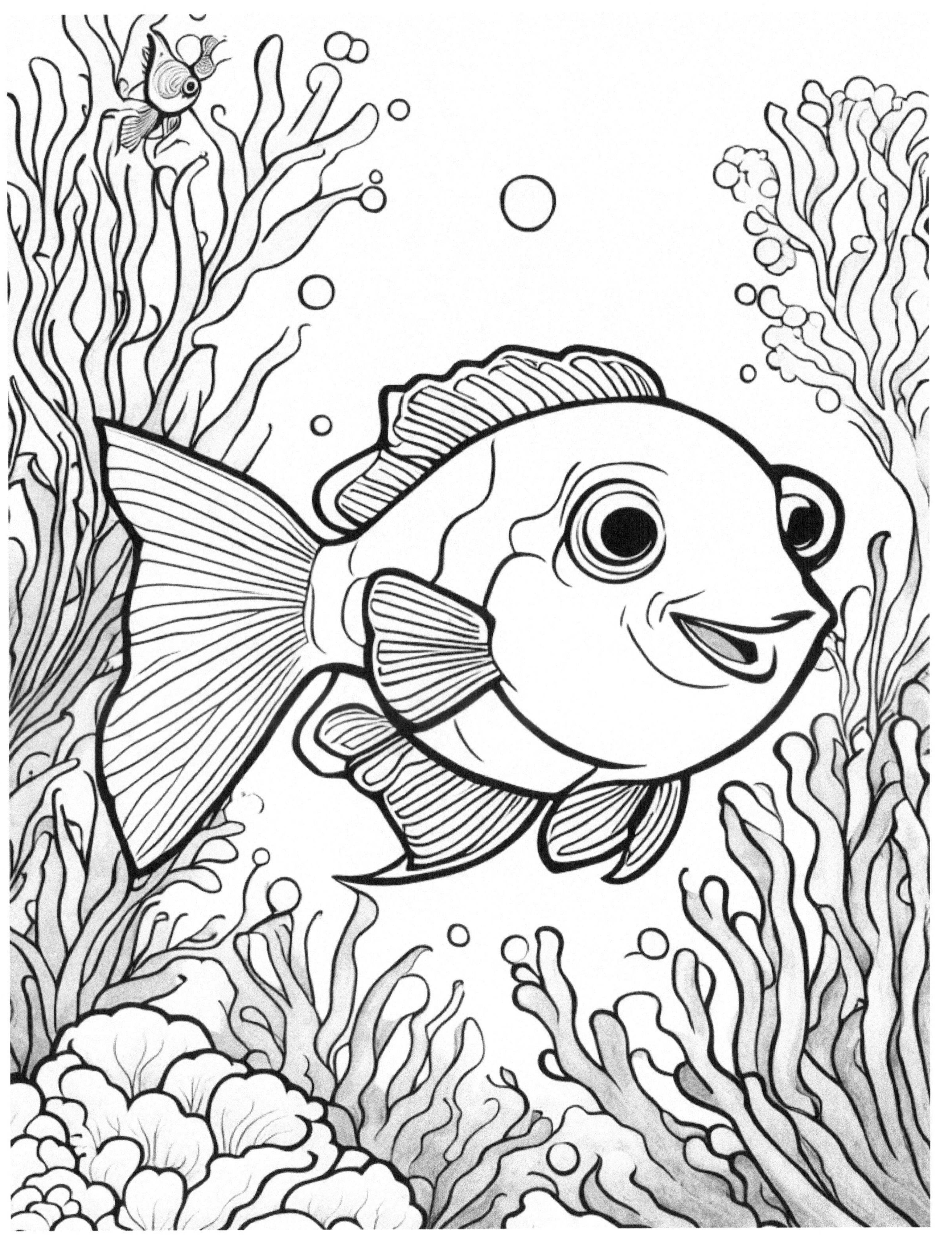

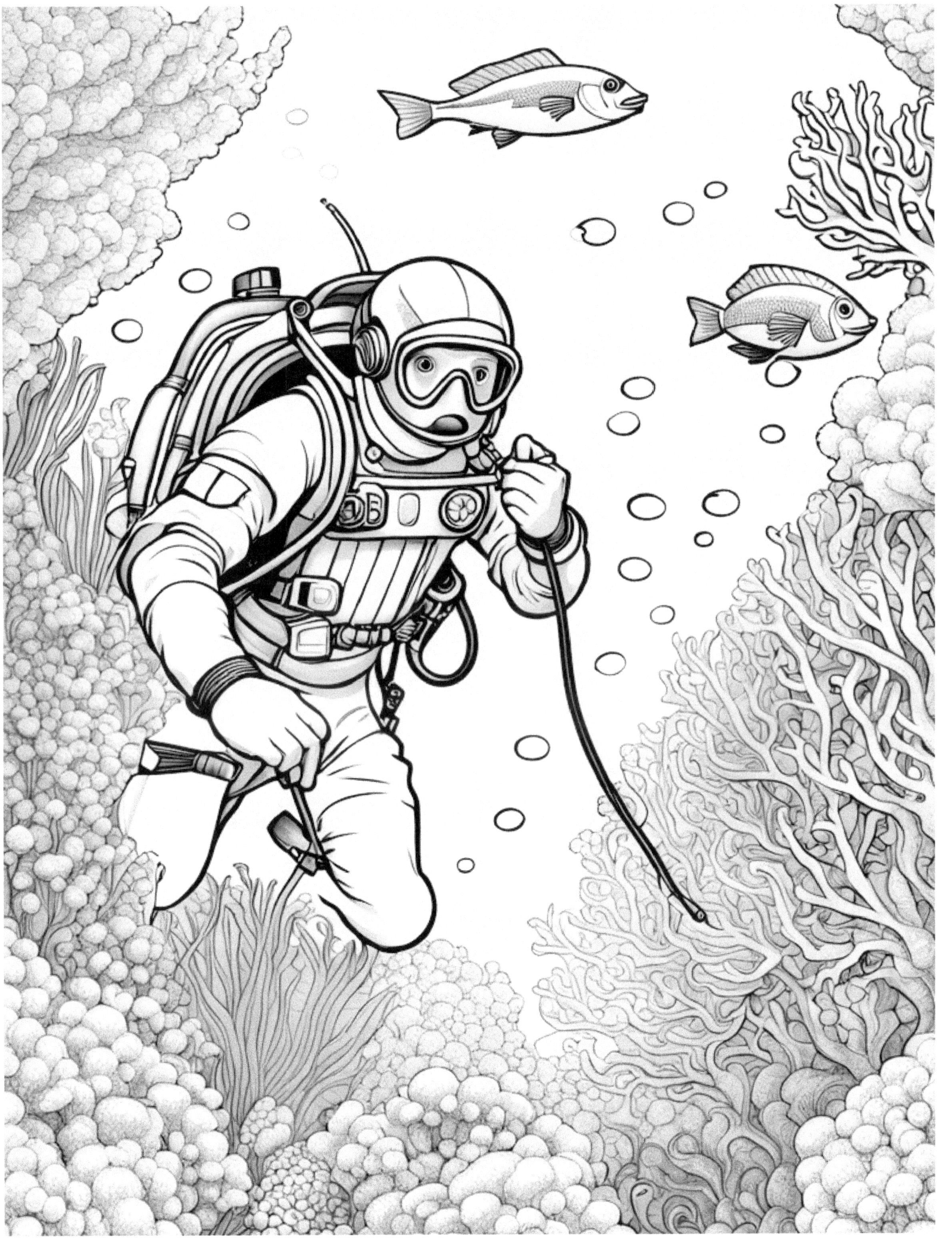

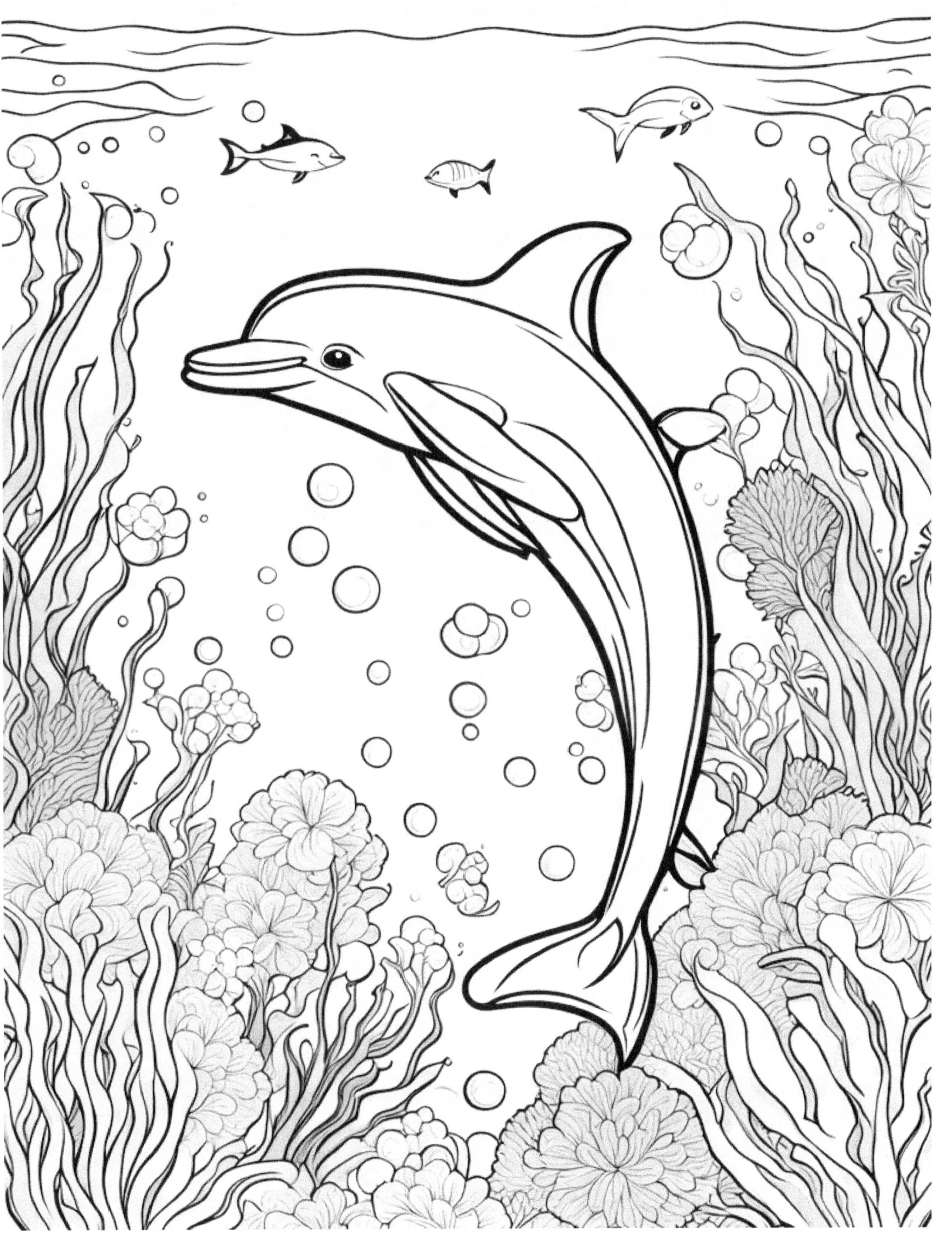

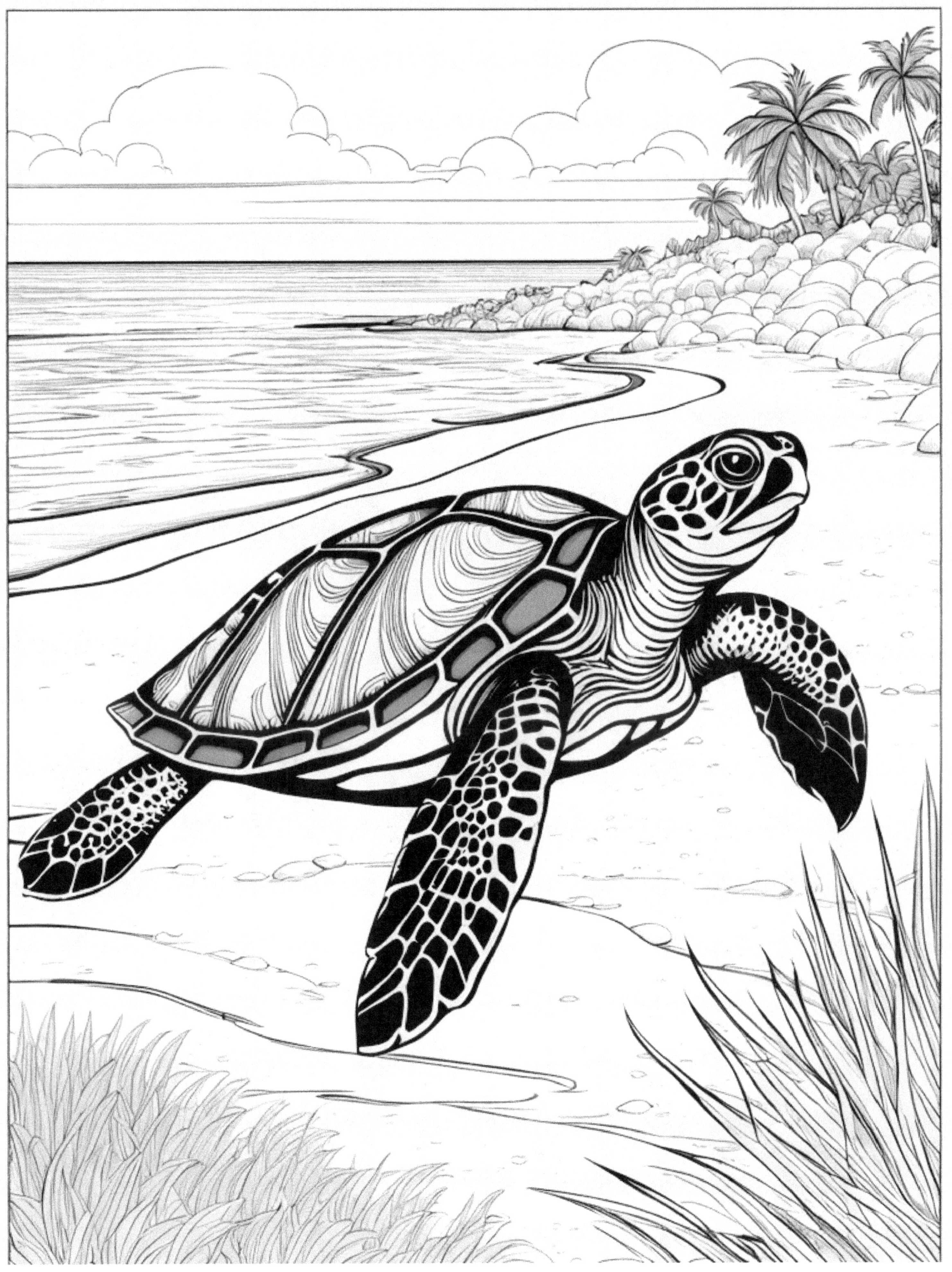

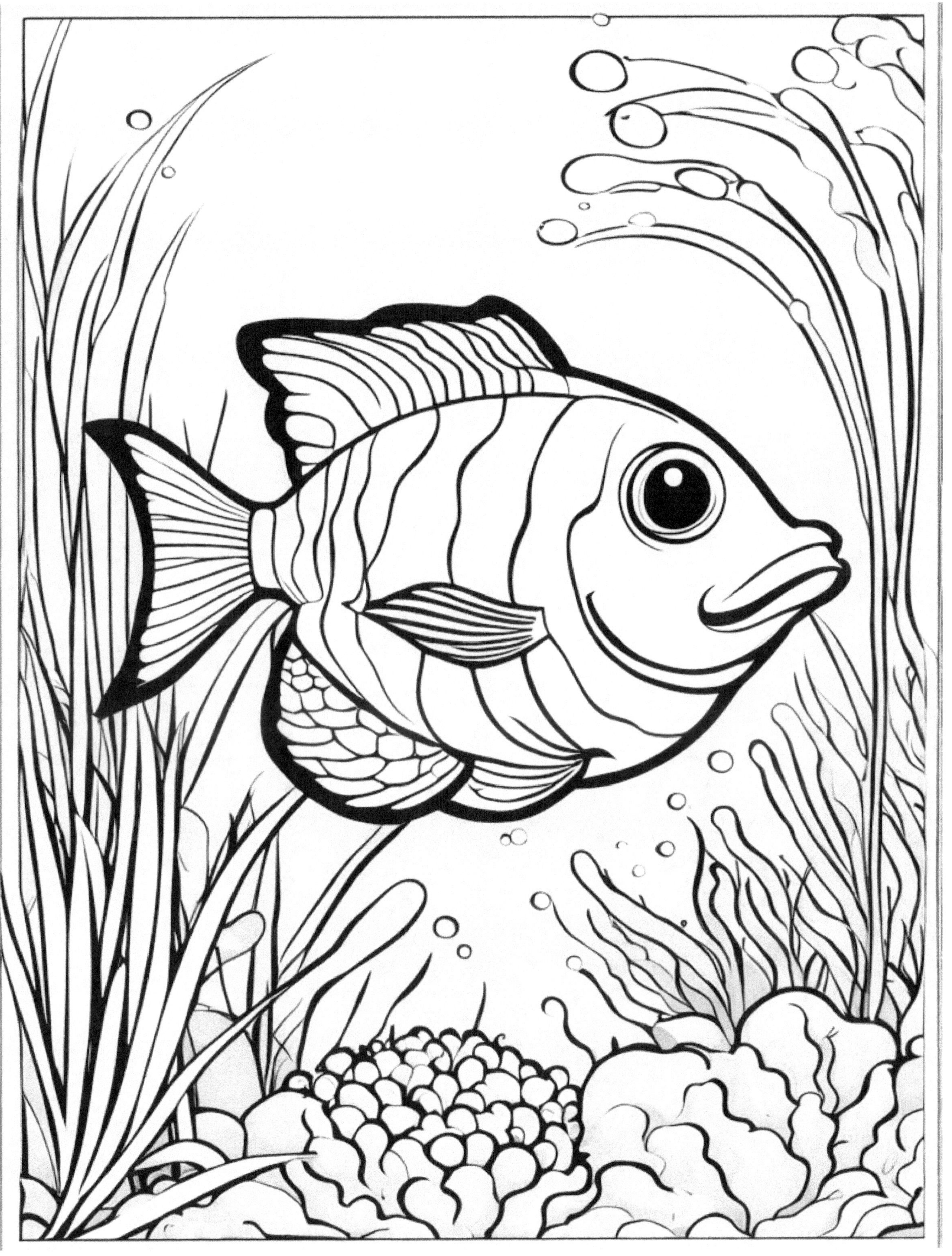

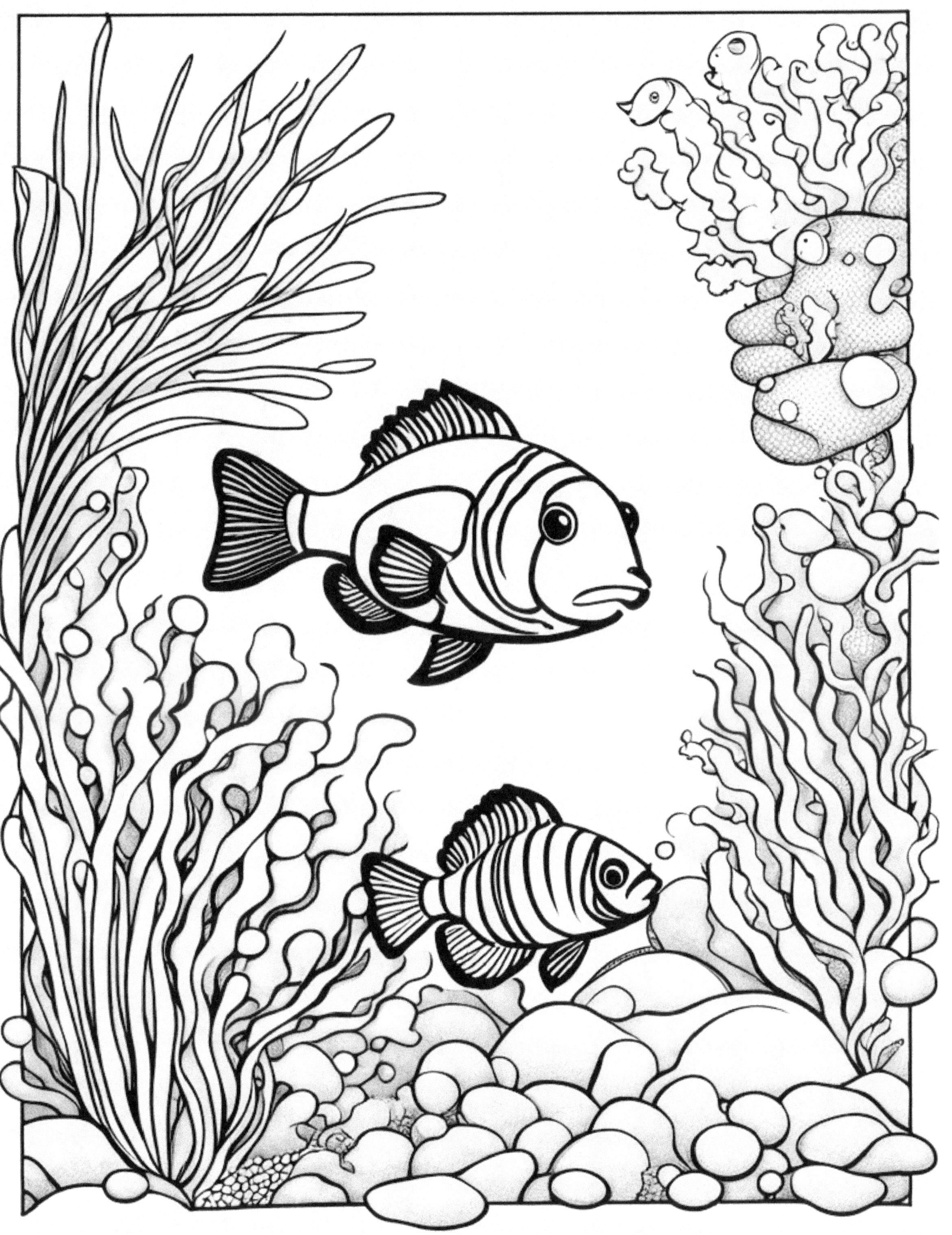